Mommy Has Cancer

ISBN 978-1-0980-4869-3 (paperback)
ISBN 978-1-0980-6471-6 (hardcover)
ISBN 978-1-0980-4870-9 (digital)

Christian Faith Publishing, Inc.
832 Park Avenue
Meadville, PA 16335
www.christianfaithpublishing.com

Printed in the United States of America

Mommy Has Cancer

What I Learned about Cancer,
and How I Helped My Mommy

Corey L. Stevenson Jr.

H

i, my name is Corey, and I am nine years old. I have two little sisters that are five years old, Kennedi and Aaliyah. They are twins.

One day my Mommy and Daddy sat me down to talk. They told me they had something very important to talk about and that I could ask any questions that I wanted to ask.

Mommy told me that there were these things in our bodies called cells, and they work to keep us healthy and strong. Some of mommy's cells were not working that well. The cells in Mommy's body did not form correctly, and they had caused something called breast cancer. She had already been to doctors, and they were going to help Mommy get the bad cells out and make cancer go away.

Daddy told me that everything would be okay, but that Mommy might begin to look different and become really sick and may become really tired. He said that she might not be able to do all the things that she usually did like take me to school, make dinner, or come to some of my football and soccer games. At first I didn't understand. I was very sad and very scared. I didn't want my Mommy to miss my games because I'm an excellent player. And most of all, I didn't want her to feel bad or become sick.

Mommy said she would have to start something called chemotherapy. She said she would have to go to the hospital to get medicine every week on a specific day. She also told me that the chemotherapy medicine would probably make her lose her hair. She told me that she would also need to have surgery and something called radiation.

Daddy told me I have an important job of helping him with Mommy when she didn't feel well and with my sisters because they can be a handful. It was a big job, but I was happy Mommy and Daddy thought I would be good at helping and being an awesome big brother. I'd show my sisters the ropes!

A little while after that, Mommy started getting chemotherapy, and her hair started to fall out. Mommy said that it hurt when her hair started falling out and that she didn't want to see her hair leave that way, so Daddy helped her cut it all off. Her hair was shorter than mine.

I was kind of nervous when Daddy cut Mommy's hair, but when I looked at Mommy and she smiled at me, it made me feel better. And guess what, Mommy was still beautiful even without her hair. Daddy kissed Mommy's head, and my sisters and I gave Mommy a big hug for being so brave. One of my sisters even asked if she could cut her hair too, but Mommy said no.

Mommy's chemotherapy made her really sick. She had a hard time walking and moved really slowly. When I saw Mommy trying to go places, I would help her like I saw Daddy help. We held her hand and walked beside her when she would go up or down the stairs, and we would bring her water to bed and sometimes food. We helped her to the bathroom, and when she would cry, we would sit with her and dry her tears. Daddy did that the best. When Mommy had awful days, Daddy would take her to the hospital. My granny would take me to see her so that I could make sure she was okay too! Mommy always told me she loved me, that she would be okay, and gave me kisses on my forehead.

The biggest job of all was helping with my sisters. I made them cereal and made sure they had their snacks. I read them bedtime stories and helped say their prayers before bed. I always told them every morning before school to have a good day, and in the evening, I would help them with their homework. Mommy liked it when I did that, and she told me she was proud of me.

Sometimes at school, I would be sad and worried about Mommy. Mommy had told my teachers about her cancer treatments, so they would give me lots of hugs or sometimes call Mommy so that I can talk to her and be sure she's okay. Sometimes Daddy or Granny would come to check on me at school and let me know everything was going well, and Mommy would be better soon.

On Mommy's last day of chemotherapy, we had a big celebration. Mommy, my family, and lots of Mommy's friends came over and had cake and rang lots of bells. Mommy explained that this was the way we knew our journey with cancer was almost over. Mommy smiled a lot that day, and she cried lots of happy tears. Now that chemotherapy was over, Mommy had to have surgery to remove the bad cancer cells from her body.

On the day of surgery I was a little scared, but Mommy promised that she would be home from the hospital before I got back home from school but that she would have big boo-boos, so my sisters and I would have to use gentle touches for hugs and kisses. Mommy prayed with me before school and asked that God keep me safe, full of joy, and focused on my day. And He did just that.

I helped Mommy a lot more after surgery because she couldn't move around very much. I sat with her and kept her covered up while she slept and got her water to drink when it was time to take medicine. I felt like a doctor, and Mommy was an excellent patient.

When Mommy started to feel better, she was able to come to my football practices and games! That made me so happy. Mommy is a loud cheerer! At my last game of the season, Mommy was there and she got to see me get my medal. She took lots of pictures, and I could tell she was proud of me. After the games, Mommy always calls all of my uncles, aunts, and cousins to report how many touchdowns I scored. I think it's pretty funny.

Very soon, Mommy started radiation. She said this would be a bunch of doctors' appointments where she would have laser pointed at her underarm and chest to make sure other cancer cells don't come back. She said that the radiation might make her tired, but it wouldn't be like chemotherapy. Even when Mommy was tired, it didn't stop her. She still took me to school and sometimes picked me up too. She came to my class parties and met all of my teachers.

Mommy encouraged me to start public speaking at school, and I became a lighthouse leader. That means that I got to make announcements on the loudspeaker and have speaking parts in school assemblies.

On Veterans Day, Mommy rushed from her radiation appointment to hear me make my first big speech in a school assembly. I was very nervous because there were lots of people and lots of veterans, like my dad. After my speech, I knew I had done a great job. I knew because Mommy was crying and the school even asked to interview me and my mom and dad for our school newspaper.

I learned a lot when Mommy had cancer. I learned to be a great big brother and how to help around the house. I learned more about God and that He kept watching over us and helped Mommy get better again. I learned about chemotherapy, radiation and how important it is take care of others and ourselves. I learned that Mommy loves me, my sisters, and my daddy more than anything in this world and that she is really strong.

I love my Mommy. I think she's the best Mommy in the world, and I'm so proud of her for being brave, and she kicked cancer's butt. I also learned I'm pretty brave, too!

About the Author

Corey L. Stevenson Jr. is the author behind *Mommy Has Cancer*. This nine-year-old from St. Louis Missouri desired to help other children understand the importance of being a big helper and supporter of parents that may go through a cancer journey.

Corey is a brave and loving big brother to twin sisters Kennedi and Aaliyah and awesome son to mom, Anastasia R. Stevenson (survivor, stage 2B breast cancer), and dad, Corey L. Stevenson Sr. Corey is a lighthouse leader at the school he attends in St. Louis and will continue his author journey to seek out the stories that need to be told.

CPSIA information can be obtained
at www.ICGtesting.com
Printed in the USA
LVHW021218240621
691048LV00006B/170